God's Mercy Endures Forever

Guidelines
on the Presentation
of Jews and Judaism
in Catholic Preaching

September 1988

Bishops' Committee on the Liturgy
National Conference of Catholic Bishops

In its planning documents for the years 1986 and 1987 the Bishops' Committee on the Liturgy was authorized to prepare a statement and a set of guidelines concerning the presentation of Jews and Judaism in Catholic preaching in response to the 1985 *Notes on the Correct Way to Present the Jews and Judaism in Preaching and Catechesis of the Roman Catholic Church* issued by the Holy See's Commission for Religious Relations with the Jews. The present document, *God's Mercy Endures Forever: Guidelines on the Presentation of Jews and Judaism in Catholic Preaching,* after consultation with the Bishops' Committee for Ecumenical and Interreligious Affairs, was approved by the Bishops' Committee on the Liturgy in June 1987, reviewed by the Administrative Committee of the National Conference of Catholic Bishops on September 13, 1988, and is authorized for publication by the undersigned as a statement of the Bishops' Committee on the Liturgy.

September 28, 1988

Monsignor Daniel F. Hoye
General Secretary
NCCB/USCC

ISBN 1-55586-247-0

Copyright © 1988
United States Catholic Conference, Inc.
Washington, D.C.
All rights reserved.

CONTENTS

Preface
  Most Reverend Joseph P. Delaney / 1

Introduction / 3

Jewish Roots of the Liturgy / 4

Historical Perspectives and Contemporary Proclamation / 5

Advent: The Relationship between the Scriptures / 7

Lent: Controversies and Conflicts / 9

Holy Week: The Passion Narratives / 11

The Easter Season / 13

Pastoral Activity during Holy Week and the Easter Season / 13

Preaching throughout the Year / 15

Suggested Reading / 17

Give thanks to the LORD, for he is good,
   for his mercy endures forever;
Give thanks to the God of gods,
   for his mercy endures forever;
Give thanks to the Lord of lords,
   for his mercy endures forever;

• • • • •

Who remembered us in our abjection,
   for his mercy endures forever;
And freed us from our foes,
   for his mercy endures forever;
Who gives food to all flesh,
   for his mercy endures forever.
Give thanks to the God of heaven,
   for his mercy endures forever.

Psalm 136:1-3, 23-26

Preface

Even in the twentieth century, the age of the Holocaust, the Shoah, the "Scouring Wind," God's mercy endures forever.

The Holocaust drew its fiery breath from the ancient, sometimes latent, but always persistent anti-Semitism which, over the centuries, found too large a place within the hearts of too many Christian men and women. Yet, since the Holocaust and since the Second Vatican Council, Christians have struggled to learn the reasons for such irrational and anti-Christian feelings against that special people for whom "God's mercy endures forever," to deal with those feelings, and to overcome them through knowledge, understanding, dialogue, and love.

For the past fifteen years, the Bishops' Committee on the Liturgy and its Secretariat have attempted to respond to the decree of *Nostra Aetate* and to the various documents issued by the Holy See's Commission for Religious Relations with the Jews, to see to it that our liturgical celebrations never again become occasions for that anti-Semitic or anti-Jewish sentiment that sometimes marred the liturgy in the past. Working with the the Bishops' Committee for Ecumenical and Interreligious Affairs and the Anti-Defamation League of B'nai B'rith, the Committee on the Liturgy and its Secretariat have suggested pastoral ways to deal with such matters as Christians gathering for a seder in Holy Week, the proper understanding of the *Improperia* on Good Friday, and the proclamation of the passion nar-ratives in Holy Week, particularly on Good Friday.

The present statement and guidelines are also offered in response to *Nostra Aetate* and especially to the latest guidelines issued in 1985 by the Commission for Religious Relations with the Jews. These guidelines are intended to offer assistance to Catholic preachers so that Jews and Judaism are correctly and rightly presented in homilies and other forms of preaching. For preaching to be of the Spirit, the heart of the preacher must be converted. These guidelines are also meant to offer preachers assistance in their own understanding of Jews and Judaism and, if necessary, to be a help in their own conversion.

The preparation and publication of *God's Mercy Endures Forever* was made possible only because of the participation and insight of a number of men and women who are scholars of the Bible, of Christian and Jewish liturgy, or of Judaism. The Liturgy Committee and

Secretariat owe a special debt of gratitude to the Anti-Defamation League of B'nai B'rith and to the NCCB Secretariat for Catholic-Jewish Relations for their support and assistance at every turn in the preparation of this document, which takes its title from that *hesed*, that enduring merciful love of God for all who are faithful to the Law.

> Most Rev. Joseph P. Delaney
> Bishop of Fort Worth
> Chairman
> Bishops' Committee on the Liturgy

Introduction

On June 24, 1985, the solemnity of the Birth of John the Baptist, the Holy See's Commission for Religious Relations with the Jews issued its *Notes on the Correct Way to Present the Jews and Judaism in Preaching and Catechesis of the Roman Catholic Church* (hereafter, 1985 *Notes*; USCC Publication No. 970). The 1985 *Notes* rested on a foundation of previous church statements, addressing the tasks given Catholic homilists by the Second Vatican Council's *Declaration on the Relationship of the Church to Non-Christian Religions (Nostra Aetate)*, no. 4.

On December 1, 1974, for example, the Holy See had issued *Guidelines and Suggestions for Implementing the Conciliar Declaration "Nostra Aetate," no. 4* (hereafter, 1974 *Guidelines*). The second and third sections of this document placed central emphasis on the important and indispensable role of the homilist in ensuring that God's Word be received without prejudice toward the Jewish people or their religious traditions, asking "with respect to liturgical readings," that "care be taken to see that homilies based on them will not distort their meaning, especially when it is a question of passages which seem to show the Jewish people as such in unfavorable light" (1974 *Guidelines*, no. 2).

In this country, the National Conference of Catholic Bishops, in 1975, similarly urged catechists and homilists to work together to develop among Catholics increasing "appreciation of the Jewishness of that heritage and rich spirituality which we derive from Abraham, Moses, the prophets, the psalmists, and other spiritual giants of the Hebrew Scriptures" (*Statement on Catholic-Jewish Relations*, November 20, 1975, no. 12).

Much progress has been made since then. As it continues, sensitivities will need even further sharpening, founded on the Church's growing understanding of biblical and rabbinic Judaism.

It is the purpose of these present *Guidelines* to assist the homilist in these continuing efforts by indicating some of the major areas where challenges and opportunities occur and by offering perspectives and suggestions for dealing with them.

Jewish Roots of the Liturgy

1. "Our common spiritual heritage [with Judaism] is considerable. To assess it carefully in itself and with due awareness of the faith and religious life of the Jewish people as they are professed and practised still today, can greatly help us to understand better certain aspects of the life of the Church. Such is the case with the liturgy, whose Jewish roots remain still to be examined more deeply, and in any case should be better known and appreciated by the faithful" (Pope John Paul II, March 6, 1982).

2. Nowhere is the deep spiritual bond between Judaism and Christianity more apparent than in the liturgy. The very concepts of a liturgical cycle of feasts and the *lectio continua* principle of the lectionary that so mark Catholic tradition are adopted from Jewish liturgical practice. Easter and Pentecost have historical roots in the Jewish feasts of Passover and Shavuot. Though their Christian meaning is quite distinct, an awareness of their original context in the story of Israel is vital to their understanding, as the lectionary readings themselves suggest. Where appropriate, such relationships should be pointed out. The homilist, as a "mediator of meaning" (NCCB Committee on Priestly Life and Ministry, *Fulfilled in Your Hearing*, 1982) interprets for the liturgical assembly not only the Scriptures but their liturgical context as well.

3. The central action of Christian worship, the eucharistic celebration, is likewise linked historically with Jewish ritual. The term for Church, *ecclesia*, like the original sense of the word *synagogue*, is an equivalent for the Hebrew *keneset* or *kenessiyah* (assembly). The Christian understanding of *ecclesia* is based on the biblical understanding of *qahal* as the formal "gathering" of the people of God. The Christian *ordo* (order of worship) is an exact rendering of the earliest rabbinic idea of prayer, called a *seder*, that is, an "order" of service. Moreover, the Christian *ordo* takes its form and structure from the Jewish *seder*: the Liturgy of the Word, with its alternating biblical readings, doxologies, and blessings; and the liturgical form of the Eucharist, rooted in Jewish meal liturgy, with its blessings over bread and wine. Theologically, the Christian concept of *anamnesis* coincides with the Jewish understanding of *zikkaron* (memorial reenactment). Applied to the Passover celebration, *zikkaron* refers to the fact that God's saving deed is not only recalled but actually relived through the ritual meal. The synoptic gospels present Jesus as instituting the

Eucharist during a Passover *seder* celebrated with his followers, giving to it a new and distinctly Christian "memory."

4. In addition to the liturgical seasons and the Eucharist, numerous details of prayer forms and ritual exemplify the Church's continuing relationship with the Jewish people through the ages. The liturgy of the hours and the formulas of many of the Church's most memorable prayers, such as the "Our Father," continue to resonate with rabbinic Judaism and contemporary synagogue prayers.

Historical Perspectives and Contemporary Proclamation

5. The strongly Jewish character of Jesus' teaching and that of the primitive Church was culturally adapted by the growing Gentile majority and later blurred by controversies alienating Christianity from emerging rabbinic Judaism at the end of the first century. "By the third century, however, a de-Judaizing process had set in which tended to undervalue the Jewish origins of the Church, a tendency that has surfaced from time to time in devious ways throughout Christian history" (*Statement on Catholic-Jewish Relations*, no. 12).

6. This process has manifested itself in various ways in Christian history. In the second century, Marcion carried it to its absurd extreme, teaching a complete opposition between the Hebrew and Christian Scriptures and declaring that different Gods had inspired the two Testaments. Despite the Church's condemnation of Marcion's teachings, some Christians over the centuries continued to dichotomize the Bible into two mutually contradictory parts. They argued, for example, that the New Covenant "abrogated" or "superseded" the Old, and that the Sinai Covenant was discarded by God and replaced with another. The Second Vatican Council, in *Dei Verbum* and *Nostra Aetate*, rejected these theories of the relationship between the Scriptures. In a major address in 1980, Pope John Paul II linked the renewed understanding of Scripture with the Church's understanding of its relationship with the Jewish people, stating that the dialogue, as "the meeting between the people of God of the Old Covenant, never revoked by God, is at the same time a dialogue within our Church, that is to say, a dialogue between the first and second part of its Bible" (Pope John Paul II, Mainz, November 17, 1980).

7. Another misunderstanding rejected by the Second Vatican Council was the notion of collective guilt, which charged the Jewish people *as a whole* with responsibility for Jesus' death (cf. nos. 21-25 below, on

Holy Week). From the theory of collective guilt, it followed for some that Jewish suffering over the ages reflected divine retribution on the Jews for an alleged "deicide." While both rabbinic Judaism and early Christianity saw in the destruction of the Jerusalem Temple in A.D. 70 a sense of divine punishment (see Lk 19:42-44), the theory of collective guilt went well beyond Jesus' poignant expression of his love as a Jew for Jerusalem and the destruction it would face at the hands of Imperial Rome. Collective guilt implied that because "the Jews" had rejected Jesus, God had rejected them. With direct reference to Luke 19:44, the Second Vatican Council reminded Catholics that "nevertheless, now as before, God holds the Jews most dear for the sake of their fathers; he does not repent of the gifts he makes or of the calls he issues," and established as an overriding hermeneutical principle for homilists dealing with such passages that "the Jews should not be represented as rejected by God or accursed, as if this followed from Holy Scripture" (*Nostra Aetate*, no. 4; cf. 1985 *Notes*, VI:33).

8. Reasons for increased sensitivity to the ways in which Jews and Judaism are presented in homilies are multiple. First, understanding of the biblical readings and of the structure of Catholic liturgy will be enhanced by an appreciation of their ancient sources and their continuing spiritual links with Judaism. The Christian proclamation of the saving deeds of the One God through Jesus was formed in the context of Second Temple Judaism and cannot be understood thoroughly without that context. It is a proclamation that, at its heart, stands in solidarity with the continuing Jewish witness in affirming the One God as Lord of history. Further, false or demeaning portraits of a repudiated Israel may undermine Christianity as well. How can one confidently affirm the truth of God's covenant with all humanity and creation in Christ (see Rom 8:21) without at the same time affirming God's faithfulness to the Covenant with Israel that also lies at the heart of the biblical testimony?

9. As Catholic homilists know, the liturgical year presents both opportunities and challenges. One can show the parallels between the Jewish and Catholic liturgical cycles. And one can, with clarity, confront misinterpretations of the meaning of the lectionary readings, which have been too familiar in the past. Specifically, homilists can guide people away from a triumphalism that would equate the pilgrim Church with the Reign of God, which is the Church's mission to herald and proclaim. Likewise, homilists can confront the unconscious transmission of anti-Judaism through cliches that derive from an unhistorical overgeneralization of the self-critical aspects of the story

of Israel as told in the Scriptures (e.g., "hardheartedness" of the Jews, "blindness," "legalism," "materialism," "rejection of Jesus," etc.). From Advent through Passover/Easter, to Yom Kippur and Rosh Hashana, the Catholic and Jewish liturgical cycles spiral around one another in a stately progression of challenges to God's people to repent, to remain faithful to God's call, and to prepare the world for the coming of God's Reign. While each is distinct and unique, they are related to one another. Christianity is engrafted on and continues to draw sustenance from the common root, biblical Israel (Rom 11:13-24).

10. In this respect, the 1985 *Notes*, stressing "the unity of the divine plan" (no. 11), caution against a simplistic framing of the relationship of Christianity and Judaism as "two parallel ways of salvation" (no. 7). The Church proclaims the universal salvific significance of the Christ-event and looks forward to the day when "there shall be one flock and one shepherd" (Jn 10:16; cf. Is 66:2; Zep 3:9; Jer 23:3; Ez 11:17; see also no. 31e below). So intimate is this relationship that the Church "encounters the mystery of Israel" when "pondering her own mystery" (1974 *Guidelines*, no. 5).

Advent: The Relationship between the Scriptures

11. The lectionary readings from the prophets are selected to bring out the ancient Christian theme that Jesus is the "fulfillment" of the biblical message of hope and promise, the inauguration of the "days to come" described, for example, by the daily Advent Masses, and on Sundays by Isaiah in cycle A and Jeremiah in cycle C for the First Sunday of Advent. This truth needs to be framed very carefully. Christians believe that Jesus is the promised Messiah who has come (see Lk 4:22), but also know that his messianic kingdom is not yet fully realized. The ancient messianic prophecies are not merely temporal predictions but profound expressions of eschatological hope. Since this dimension can be misunderstood or even missed altogether, the homilist needs to raise clearly the hope found in the prophets and heightened in the proclamation of Christ. This hope includes trust in what is promised but not yet seen. While the biblical prophecies of an age of universal *shalom* are "fulfilled" (i.e., irreversibly inaugurated) in Christ's coming, that fulfillment is not yet completely worked out in each person's life or perfected in the world at large (1974 *Guidelines*, no. 2). It is the mission of the Church, as also that of the Jewish people, to proclaim and to work to prepare the world for the full flowering of God's Reign, which is, but is "not yet" (cf. 1974 *Guidelines*, II). Both the Christian "Our Father" and the Jewish *Kaddish* exemplify this

message. Thus, both Christianity and Judaism seal their worship with a common hope: "Thy kingdom come!"

12. Christians proclaim that the Messiah has indeed come and that God's Reign is "at hand." With the Jewish people, we await the complete realization of the messianic age.

> In underlining the eschatological dimension of Christianity, we shall reach a greater awareness that the people of God of the Old and the New Testament are tending toward a like end in the future: the coming or return of the Messiah--even if they start from two different points of view (1985 *Notes*, nos. 18-19).

13. Other difficulties may be less theologically momentous but can still be troublesome. For example, the reading from Baruch in cycle C or from Isaiah in cycle A for the Second Sunday of Advent can leave the impression that pre-Jesus Israel was wholly guilt-ridden and in mourning, and Judaism virtually moribund. In fact, in their original historical settings, such passages reveal Judaism's remarkable capacity for self-criticism. While Israel had periods of deep mourning (see Lamentations) and was justly accused of sinfulness (e.g., see Jeremiah), it also experienced periods of joy, return from Exile, and continuing *teshuvah*, turning back to God in faithful repentance. Judaism was and is incredibly complex and vital, with a wide variety of creative spiritual movements vying for the people's adherence.

14. The reform of the liturgy initiated by the Second Vatican Council reintroduced regular readings from the Old Testament into the lectionary. For Catholics, the Old Testament is that collection that contains the Hebrew Scriptures and the seven deuterocanonical books. Using postbiblical Jewish sources, with respect for the essential differences between Christian and Jewish traditions of biblical interpretation, can enliven the approach to the biblical text (cf. nos. 31a and 31i below). The opportunity also presents a challenge for the homilist. Principles of selection of passages vary. Sometimes the readings are cyclic, providing a continuity of narrative over a period of time. At other times, especially during Advent and Lent, a reading from the prophets or one of the historical books of the Old Testament and a gospel pericope are "paired," based on such liturgical traditions as the *sensus plenior* (fuller meaning) or, as is especially the case in Ordinary Time, according to the principle of *typology*, in which biblical figures and events are seen as "types" prefiguring Jesus (see no. 31e below).

15. Many of these pairings represent natural associations of similar events and teachings. Others rely on New Testament precedent and interpretation of the messianic psalms and prophetic passages. Matthew 1:23, for example, quotes the Septuagint, which translates the Hebrew *almah* (young woman) as the Greek for *virgin* in its rendering of Isaiah 7:14. The same biblical text, therefore, can have more than one valid hermeneutical interpretation, ranging from its original historical context and intent to traditional Christological applications. The 1985 *Notes* describe this phenomenon as flowing from the "unfathomable riches" and "inexhaustible content" of the Hebrew Bible. For Christians, the unity of the Bible depends on understanding all Scripture in the light of Christ. Typology is one form, rooted in the New Testament itself, of expressing this unity of Scripture and of the divine plan (see no. 31e below). As such, it "should not lead us to forget that it [the Hebrew Bible] retains its own value as Revelation that the New Testament often does no more than resume" (1985 *Notes,* no. 15; cf. *Dei Verbum,* 14-18).

Lent: Controversies and Conflicts

16. The Lenten lectionary presents just as many challenges. Prophetic texts such as Joel (Ash Wednesday), Jeremiah's "new covenant" (cycle B, Fifth Sunday), and Isaiah (cycle C, Fifth Sunday) call the assembly to proclaim Jesus as the Christ while avoiding negativism toward Judaism.

17. In addition, many of the New Testament texts, such as Matthew's references to "hypocrites in the synagogue" (Ash Wednesday), John's depiction of Jesus in the Temple (cycle B, Third Sunday), and Jesus' conflicts with the Pharisees (e.g., Lk, cycle C, Fourth Sunday) can give the impression that the Judaism of Jesus' day was devoid of spiritual depth and essentially at odds with Jesus' teaching. References to earlier divine punishments of the Jews (e.g., 1 Cor, cycle C, Third Sunday) can further intensify a false image of Jews and Judaism as a people rejected by God.

18. In fact, however, as the 1985 *Notes* are at pains to clarify (sec. III and IV), Jesus was observant of the Torah (e.g., in the details of his circumcision and purification given in Lk 2:21-24), he extolled respect for it (see Mt 5:17-20), and he invited obedience to it (see Mt 8:4). Jesus taught in the synagogues (see Mt 4:23 and 9:35; Lk 4:15-18; Jn 18:20) and in the Temple, which he frequented, as did the disciples even after the Resurrection (see Acts 2:46; 3:1ff). While Jesus showed uniqueness and

authority in his interpretation of God's word in the Torah—in a manner that scandalized some Jews and impressed others—he did not oppose it, nor did he wish to abrogate it.

19. Jesus was perhaps closer to the Pharisees in his religious vision than to any other group of his time. The 1985 *Notes* suggest that this affinity with Pharisaism may be a reason for many of his apparent controversies with them (see no. 27). Jesus shared with the Pharisees a number of distinctive doctrines: the resurrection of the body; forms of piety such as almsgiving, daily prayer, and fasting; the liturgical practice of addressing God as Father; and the priority of the love commandment (see no. 25). Many scholars are of the view that Jesus was not so much arguing against "the Pharisees" as a group, as he was condemning excesses of some Pharisees, excesses of a sort that can be found among some Christians as well. In some cases, Jesus appears to have been participating in internal Pharisaic debates on various points of interpretation of God's law. In the case of divorce (see Mk 10:2-12), an issue that was debated hotly between the Pharisaic schools of Hillel and Shammai, Jesus goes beyond even the more stringent position of the House of Shammai. In other cases, such as the rejection of a literal interpretation of the *lex talionis* ("An eye for an eye. . . ."), Jesus' interpretation of biblical law is similar to that found in some of the prophets and ultimately adopted by rabbinic tradition as can be seen in the *Talmud*.

20. After the Church had distanced itself from Judaism (cf. no. 5 above), it tended to telescope the long historical process whereby the gospels were set down some generations after Jesus' death. Thus, certain controversies that may actually have taken place between church leaders and rabbis toward the end of the first century were "read back" into the life of Jesus:

> Some [New Testament] references hostile or less than favorable to Jews have their historical context in conflicts between the nascent Church and the Jewish community. Certain controversies reflect Christian-Jewish relations long after the time of Jesus. To establish this is of capital importance if we wish to bring out the meaning of certain gospel texts for the Christians of today. All this should be taken into account when preparing catechesis and homilies for the weeks of Lent and Holy Week (1985 *Notes*, no. 29; see no. 26 below).

Holy Week: The Passion Narratives

21. Because of the tragic history of the "Christ-killer" charge as providing a rallying cry for anti-Semites over the centuries, a strong and careful homiletic stance is necessary to combat its lingering effects today. Homilists and catechists should seek to provide a proper context for the proclamation of the passion narratives. A particularly useful and detailed discussion of the theological and historical principles involved in presentations of the passions can be found in *Criteria for the Evaluation of Dramatizations of the Passion* issued by the Bishops' Committee for Ecumenical and Interreligious Affairs (March 1988).

22. The message of the liturgy in proclaiming the passion narratives in full is to enable the assembly to see vividly the love of Christ for each person, despite their sins, a love that even death could not vanquish. "Christ in his boundless love freely underwent his passion and death because of the sins of all so that all might attain salvation" (*Nostra Aetate,* no. 4). To the extent that Christians over the centuries made Jews the scapegoat for Christ's death, they drew themselves away from the paschal mystery. For it is only by dying to one's sins that we can hope to rise with Christ to new life. This is a central truth of the Catholic faith stated by the *Catechism* of the Council of Trent in the sixteenth century and reaffirmed by the 1985 *Notes* (no. 30).

23. It is necessary to remember that the passion narratives do not offer eyewitness accounts or a modern transcript of historical events. Rather, the events have had their meaning focused, as it were, through the four theological "lenses" of the gospels. By comparing what is shared and what distinguishes the various gospel accounts from each other, the homilist can discern the core from the particular optics of each. One can then better see the significant theological differences between the passion narratives. These differences also are part of the inspired Word of God.

24. Certain historical essentials are shared by all four accounts: a growing hostility against Jesus on the part of some Jewish religious leaders (note that the Synoptic gospels do not mention the Pharisees as being involved in the events leading to Jesus' death, but only the "chief priests, scribes, and elders"); the Last Supper with the disciples; betrayal by Judas; arrest outside the city (an action conducted covertly by the Roman and Temple authorities because of Jesus' popularity among his fellow Jews); interrogation before a high priest (not

necessarily a Sanhedrin trial); formal condemnation by Pontius Pilate (cf. the Apostles' and Nicene Creeds, which mention *only* Pilate, even though some Jews were involved); crucifixion by Roman soldiers; affixing the title "King of the Jews" on the cross; death; burial; and resurrection. Many other elements, such as the crowds shouting "His blood be on us and on our children" in Matthew, or the generic use of the term "the Jews" in John, are unique to a given author and must be understood within the context of that author's overall theological scheme. Often, these unique elements reflect the perceived needs and emphases of the author's particular community at the end of the first century, *after* the split between Jews and Christians was well underway. The bitterness toward synagogue Judaism seen in John's gospel (e.g., Jn 9:22;16:2) most likely reflects the bitterness felt by John's own community after its "parting of the ways" with the Jewish community, and the martyrdom of St. Stephen illustrates that verbal disputes could, at times, lead to violence by Jews against fellow Jews who believed in Jesus.

25. Christian reflection on the passion should lead to a deep sense of the need for reconciliation with the Jewish community today. Pope John Paul II has said:

> Considering history in the light of the principles of faith in God, we must also reflect on the catastrophic event of the *Shoah*. . . .
> Considering this mystery of the suffering of Israel's children, their witness of hope, of faith, and of humanity under dehumanizing outrages, the Church experiences ever more deeply her common bond with the Jewish people and with their treasure of spiritual riches in the past and in the present" (*Address to Jewish Leadership*, Miami, September 11, 1987).

The Easter Season

26. The readings of the Easter season, especially those from the book of Acts, which is used extensively throughout this liturgical period, require particular attention from the homilist in light of the enduring bond between Jews and Christians. Some of these readings from Acts (e.g., cycles A and B for the Third and Fourth Sundays of Easter) can leave an impression of collective Jewish responsibility for the crucifixion ("You put to death the author of life...." Acts 3:15). In such cases, the homilist should put before the assembly the teachings of *Nostra Aetate* in this regard (see no. 22 above), as well as the fact noted in Acts 3:17 that what was done by some individual Jews was done "out of ignorance" so that no unwarranted conclusion about collective guilt is drawn by the hearers. The Acts may be dealing with a reflection of the Jewish-Christian relationship as it existed toward the end of the first century (when Acts was composed) rather than with the actual attitudes of the post-Easter Jerusalem Church. Homilists should desire to convey the spirit and enthusiasm of the early Church that marks these Easter season readings. But in doing so, statements about Jewish responsibility have to be kept in context. This is part of the reconciliation between Jews and Christians to which we are all called.

Pastoral Activity during Holy Week and the Easter Season

27. Pope John Paul II's visit to the Chief Rabbi of Rome on Good Friday, 1987, gives a lead for pastoral activities during Holy Week in local churches. Some dioceses and parishes, for example, have begun traditions such as holding a "Service of Reconciliation" with Jews on Palm Sunday, or inviting Holocaust survivors to address their congregations during Lent.

28. It is becoming familiar in many parishes and Catholic homes to participate in a Passover Seder during Holy Week. This practice can have educational and spiritual value. It is wrong, however, to "baptize" the Seder by ending it with New Testament readings about the Last Supper or, worse, turn it into a prologue to the Eucharist. Such mergings distort both traditions. The following advice should prove useful:

> When Christians celebrate this sacred feast among themselves, the rites of the *haggadah* for the seder should be respected in all their integrity. The seder . . . should be celebrated in a dignified manner and with sensitivity to those to whom the

seder truly belongs. The primary reason why Christians may celebrate the festival of Passover should be to acknowledge common roots in the history of salvation. Any sense of "restaging" the Last Supper of the Lord Jesus should be avoided. . . . The rites of the Triduum are the [Church's] annual memorial of the events of Jesus' dying and rising (Bishops' Committee on the Liturgy *Newsletter*, March 1980, p. 12).

Seders arranged at or in cooperation with local synagogues are encouraged.

29. Also encouraged are joint memorial services commemorating the victims of the *Shoah* (Holocaust). These should be prepared for with catechetical and adult education programming to ensure a proper spirit of shared reverence. Addressing the Jewish community of Warsaw, Pope John Paul II stressed the uniqueness and significance of Jewish memory of the *Shoah*: "More than anyone else, it is precisely you who have become this saving warning. I think that in this sense you continue your particular vocation, showing yourselves to be still the heirs of that election to which God is faithful. This is your mission in the contemporary world before . . . all of humanity" (Warsaw, June 14, 1987). On the Sunday closest to *Yom ha Shoah,* Catholics should pray for the victims of the Holocaust and their survivors. The following serve as examples of petitions for the general intercessions at Mass:

- For the victims of the Holocaust, their families, and all our Jewish brothers and sisters, that the violence and hatred they experienced may never again be repeated, we pray to the Lord.

- For the Church, that the Holocaust may be a reminder to us that we can never be indifferent to the sufferings of others, we pray to the Lord.

- For our Jewish brothers and sisters, that their confidence in the face of long-suffering may spur us on to a greater faith and trust in God, we pray to the Lord.

Preaching throughout the Year

30. The challenges that peak in the seasons of Advent, Lent, and Easter are present throughout the year in the juxtaposition of the lectionary readings. There are many occasions when it is difficult to avoid a reference either to Jews or Judaism in a homily based upon a text from the Scriptures. For all Scripture, including the New Testament, deals with Jews and Jewish themes.

31. Throughout the year, the following general principles will be helpful:

a) Consistently affirm the value of the whole Bible. While "among all the Scriptures, even those of the New Testament, the Gospels have a special preeminence" (*Dei Verbum*, 18), the Hebrew Scriptures are the word of God and have validity and dignity in and of themselves (ibid., 15). Keep in view the intentions of the biblical authors (ibid., 19).

b) Place the typology inherent in the lectionary in a proper context, neither overemphasizing nor avoiding it. Show that the meaning of the Hebrew Scriptures for their original audience is not limited to nor diminished by New Testament applications (1985 *Notes*, II).

c) Communicate a reverence for the Hebrew Scriptures and avoid approaches that reduce them to a propaedeutic or background for the New Testament. It is God who speaks, communicating himself through divine revelation (*Dei Verbum*, 6).

d) Show the connectedness between the Scriptures. The Hebrew Bible and the Jewish tradition founded on it must not be set against the New Testament in such a way that the former seems to constitute a religion of only retributive justice, fear, and legalism, with no appeal to love of God and neighbor (cf. Dt 6:5; Lv 19:18,32; Hos 11:1-9; Mt 22:34-40).

e) Enliven the eschatological hope, the "not yet" aspect of the *kerygma*. The biblical promises are realized in Christ. But the Church awaits their perfect fulfillment in Christ's glorious return when all creation is made free (1974 *Guidelines*, II).

f) Emphasize the Jewishness of Jesus and his teachings and highlight the similarities of the teachings of the Pharisees with those of Christ (1985 *Notes*, III and IV).

g) Respect the continuing validity of God's covenant with the Jewish people and their responsive faithfulness, despite centuries of suffering, to the divine call that is theirs (1985 *Notes*, VI).

h) Frame homilies to show that Christians and Jews together are "trustees and witnesses of an ethic marked by the Ten Commandments, in the observance of which humanity finds its truth and freedom" (John Paul II, Rome Synagogue, April 13, 1986).

i) Be free to draw on Jewish sources (rabbinic, medieval, and modern) in expounding the meaning of the Hebrew Scriptures and the apostolic writings. The 1974 *Guidelines* observe that "the history of Judaism did not end with the destruction of Jerusalem, but went on to develop a religious tradition . . . rich in religious values." The 1985 *Notes* (no. 14) thus speak of Christians "profiting discerningly from the traditions of Jewish readings" of the sacred texts.

32. The 1985 *Notes* describe what is central to the role of the homilist: "Attentive to the same God who has spoken, hanging on the same word, we have to witness to one same memory and one common hope in him who is master of history. We must also accept our responsibility to prepare the world for the coming of the Messiah by working together for social justice, respect for the rights of persons and nations, and for social and international reconciliation. To this we are driven, Jews and Christians, by the command to love our neighbor, by a common hope for the kingdom of God, and by the great heritage of the prophets" (1985 *Notes*, no. 19; see also Lv 19:18,32).

Suggested Reading

I. Documentation

Holy See, Commission on Religious Relations with the Jews. *Notes on the Correct Way to Present the Jews and Judaism in Preaching and Catechesis of the Roman Catholic Church.* Washington, D.C.: United States Catholic Conference (= USCC) Office of Publishing and Promotion Services, 1985.

International Catholic-Jewish Liaison Committee. *Fifteen Years of Catholic-Jewish Dialogue 1970-1985: Selected Papers.* Rome: Libreria Editrice Lateranense, 1988.

National Conference of Catholic Bishops, Committee for Ecumenical and Interreligious Affairs. *John Paul II on Jews and Judaism 1979-1986.* Eugene Fisher and Leon Klenicki, eds. Washington, D.C.: USCC Office of Publishing and Promotion Services, 1987.

_____. *Criteria for the Evaluation of Dramatizations of the Passion.* Washington, D.C.: USCC Office of Publishing and Promotion Services, 1988.

National Conference of Catholic Bishops, Committee on the Liturgy. "Celebrating the Passover Seder," *Bishops' Committee on the Liturgy Newsletter* (March 1980).

_____. "Good Friday Reproaches *(Improperia),*" *Bishops' Committee on the Liturgy Newsletter* (March 1980).

_____. *(Alternative) Reproaches for Use during the Veneration of the Cross: Good Friday.* Minister's and People's editions. Washington, D.C.: USCC Office of Publishing and Promotion Services, 1981.

_____. "Days of Remembrance of the Victims of the Holocaust," *Bishops' Committee on the Liturgy Newsletter* (March 1988).

Second Vatican Ecumenical Council. *Nostra Aetate,* Declaration on the Relationship of the Church to Non-Christian Religions. Vatican City: October 28, 1965.

_____. *Dei Verbum,* Dogmatic Constitution on Divine Revelation. Vatican City: November 18, 1965.

II. Articles and Books

Beckwith, R. "The Jewish Background to Christian Worship" in *The Study of Liturgy.* Jones, Wainwright and Yarnold, eds. New York: Oxford University Press, 1978, pp. 39-51.

Bouyer, L. "Jewish and Christian Liturgies" in *True Worship.* L. Sheppard, ed. Baltimore, Md.: Helicon Press, 1963, pp. 29-44.

Cunningham, Philip. *Jewish Apostle to the Gentiles: Paul as He Saw Himself.* Mystic, Conn.: Twenty-Third Publications, 1986.

Eliach, Yaffa. *Hassidic Tales of the Holocaust.* New York: Oxford University Press, 1982.

Finkel, A. and L. Frizzell, eds. *Standing Before God.* New York: KTAV, 1981.

Fisher, Eugene. *Seminary Education and Christian-Jewish Relations.* Washington, D.C.: National Catholic Educational Association, 1983.

_____, ed. *Within Context: Guidelines for Catechetical Presentation of Jews and Judaism in the New Testament.* Morristown, N.J.: Silver Burdett and Ginn, 1987.

_____, et al. *Twenty Years of Jewish-Catholic Relations.* Mahwah, N.J.: Paulist Press, 1986.

Flannery, Edward. *The Anguish of the Jews.* Mahwah, N.J.: Paulist Press, 1985.

Friedman, Philip. *Their Brothers' Keepers: Christian Heroes and Heroines Who Helped the Oppressed Escape Nazi Terror.* New York: Holocaust Library, 1978.

Harrington, Daniel, SJ. *God's People in Christ: New Testament Perspectives on the Church and Judaism.* Philadelphia: Fortress Press, 1980.

Idelsohn, A. Z. *Jewish Liturgy and Its Development.* New York: Schocken Books, 1967.

Klenicki, Leon. *The Passover Celebration.* Chicago: Liturgy Training Publications, 1980.

_____ and Eugene Fisher. *Root and Branches: Biblical Judaism, Rabbinic Judaism and Early Christianity.* Winona, Minn.: St. Mary's Press, 1987.

_____ and Gabe Huck, eds. *Spirituality and Prayer.* New York: Paulist Press, 1983.

Littell, M. S. *Liturgies on the Holocaust: An Interfaith Anthology.* Lewiston, N.Y.: Edwin Mellen Press, 1986.

Muffs, J. H., and D. B. Klein, eds. *The Holocaust in Books and Films: A Selected, Annotated List.* New York: Hippocrene Books/Anti-Defamation League, 1986.

Nickelsburg, G. and M. Stone. *Faith and Piety in Early Judaism: Texts and Documents.* Philadelphia: Fortress Press, 1983.

Pawlikowski, John T. *The Challenge of the Holocaust for Christian Theology.* New York: Anti-Defamation League, 1978.

_____ and James A. Wilde. *When Catholics Speak about Jews.* Chicago: Liturgy Training Publications, 1987.

Peli, Pinchus. *Torah Today.* Washington, D.C.: B'nai B'rith Books, 1987.

Petuchowski, Jacob and Michael Brocke. *The Lord's Prayer and Jewish Liturgy.* New York: Seabury Press, 1978.

Rittner, Carol and Sandra Myers. *The Courage to Care.* New York: New York University Press, 1986.

Saldarini, Anthony J. *Jesus and Passover.* New York: Paulist Press, 1984.

Sloyan, Gerard S. *Jesus in Focus.* Mystic, Conn.: Twenty-Third Publications, 1983.

_____."The Lectionary as a Context for Interpretation," *Interpretation* (April 1977): 131-138.

Strack, H. L. *Introduction to the Talmud and Midrash.* New York: Atheneum, 1969.

Thoma, Clemens and Michael Wyschogrod, eds. *Understanding Scripture: Explorations of Jewish and Christian Traditions of Interpretation.* New York/Mahwah: Paulist Press, 1987.

Townsend, John T. *A Liturgical Interpretation of the Passion of Jesus Christ.* New York: National Conference of Christians and Jews.

Wiesel, Elie. *Night.* New York: Avon, 1969.

_____ and Albert H. Friedlander. *The Six Days of Destruction: Meditations toward Hope.* New York/Mahwah: Paulist Press, 1988.